ATLANTIC DIET
Meal Prep

Discover Easy and Healthy Atlantic Recipes to Prep and Enjoy on the Go for Optimal Health and Vitality

Includes a 28-Day Meal Plan

DAVID THOMPSON

Copyright © 2024 by David Thompson. All Rights Reserved.

No part of this publication may be reproduced, distributed, or transmitted in any form or by any means, including photocopying, recording, or other electronic or mechanical methods, without the prior written permission of the publisher, except in the case of brief quotations embodied in critical reviews and certain other noncommercial uses permitted by copyright law.

DISCLAIMER:

The content in this cookbook is intended solely for informational purposes and, while diligence has been applied to ensure its accuracy and thoroughness, no guarantees are made regarding its completeness or reliability. Neither the author nor the publisher shall be held liable for any potential damages or losses, whether direct or incidental, that may arise from utilizing this book. It's important to note that the dietary suggestions and recipes within are not meant to serve as direct medical advice. Readers should consult healthcare professionals for personalized dietary guidance. The perspectives presented herein are those of the author alone and do not reflect the publisher's views.

CONTENTS

INTRODUCTION 5

CHAPTER 1: FOUNDATIONS OF ATLANTIC DIET MEAL PREP 7

    The Atlantic Diet and Meal Prep Essentials 7

    The Benefits of Meal Prepping 8

    Stocking Your Pantry for Success 9

CHAPTER 2: MEAL PREP STARTEGIES 11

    Setting Up Your Meal Prep Routine 11

    Creating a Balanced Meal Plan 12

    Efficient Shopping Strategies 13

    Time-Saving Cooking Techniques 14

CHAPTER 3: BREAKFAST RECIPES 17

    Smoked Salmon Avocado Toast 17

    Seafood Frittata 18

    Quinoa Berry Breakfast Bowl 19

    Sardine and Tomato on Wholegrain 20

    Mackerel and Sweet Potato Hash 21

    Oatmeal with Poached Pear 22

    Berry Chia Pudding 23

    Greek Yogurt with Honeyed Walnuts 24

    Spinach and Feta Scrambled Eggs 25

    Shrimp and Avocado Salad 26

CHAPTER 4: LUNCH RECIPES 27

    Tuna Niçoise Salad 27

    Simple Seafood Paella 28

    Salmon and Quinoa Salad 29

    Portuguese Fish Stew 30

    Crab and Avocado Wrap 31

    Lentil Salad with Cod 32

    Shrimp Mango Ceviche 33

    Grilled Sardine Bruschetta 34

Mediterranean Tuna Pasta Salad 35

Haddock in Parchment with Vegetables 36

CHAPTER 5: DINNER RECIPES 37

Baked Salmon with Roasted Veggies 37

Creamy Seafood Risotto 38

Cod in Tomato Chickpea Sauce 39

Mussels in White Wine 40

Grilled Swordfish with Quinoa 41

Sea Bass with Olive Salsa 42

Shrimp Asparagus Stir-Fry 43

Clam and Kale Soup 44

Octopus and Potato Salad 45

Herb-Crusted Hake 46

CHAPTER 6: SNACKS AND SIDES 47

Garlic Roasted Brussels Sprouts 47

Cucumber Seaweed Salad 48

Spicy Roasted Chickpeas 49

Grilled Vegetable Skewers 50

Zucchini and Corn Fritters 51

Olive and Tomato Tapenade 52

Sweet Potato Wedges with Herbs 53

Marinated Artichoke Hearts 54

CHAPTER 7: DESSERTS 55

Baked Apples with Cinnamon 55

Berry and Yogurt Parfait 56

Almond and Orange Flourless Cake 57

Dark Chocolate Sea Salt Almonds 58

Grilled Pineapple with Honey Drizzle 59

Lemon and Olive Oil Sorbet 60

Poached Pears in Red Wine 61

Fig and Ricotta Tart 62

CHAPTER 8: 28-DAY MEAL PLAN 63
Week 1 63
Week 2 64
Week 3 65
Week 4 66

CHAPTER 9: SUSTAINING THE ATLANTIC DIET LIFESTYLE 68
Beyond the 4-Week Plan... 68
Adapting Meal Prep to Life's Changes 69
Staying Motivated and Inspired 70

CHAPTER 10: CONCLUSION 72
FAQs on the Atlantic Diet 72

INTRODUCTION

Step into the world of the dieting, where meal planning becomes an art form. This book is a guide to embracing an approach to life that recognizes the abundance of the Atlantic coast, intertwining the rich traditions of its bordering cultures with the practicalities of modern-day living. The Atlantic Diet, with its emphasis on fresh seafood, abundant fruits and vegetables, whole grains, and heart-healthy fats, is more than a dietary plan; it's an approach towards greater health, sustainability, and culinary delight.

This journey begins with an awareness of the Atlantic Diet, which is deeply rooted in coastal communities that have thrived on the ocean's richness for centuries. This diet exemplifies the synergy of land and sea, where the daily catch and seasonal harvest dictate meal patterns. It is a diet known for its positive effects on health including heart health, weight management, and overall vitality, owing to its substantial amount of omega-3 fatty acids, fiber, antioxidants, and essential nutrients.

But how do we incorporate such a varied diet into our fast-paced lives? The answer is meal prep, a structured approach to food that simplifies healthy eating by planning and preparing meals in advance. This book will guide you through a 4-week meal plan that has been meticulously put together to introduce you to the diverse flavors and nutritional benefits of the Atlantic Diet. Each recipe has been chosen not only for its adherence to dietary principles but also for its ease of preparation, ensuring that healthy eating fits seamlessly into your busy schedule.

As you progress through the meal plans, you will discover energizing breakfasts, satisfying lunches, and nourishing and delightful dinners. Each meal, from the omega-rich Smoked Salmon Avocado Toast to the heartwarming Portuguese Fish Stew for lunch and the exquisite Herb-Crusted Hake to end the evening, is a step toward good health and well-being. This is also about acquiring the skills and techniques that will empower you to create nourishing dishes with the ingredients you have on hand.

What happens beyond the initial four-week plan? This book guides you to making the Atlantic Diet a permanent part of your lifestyle. It teaches you how to adjust meal planning to life's ever-changing conditions, ensuring that your dedication to health and fitness lasts through busy schedules, seasonal changes, and even those times when motivation wanes.

Flexibility, inventiveness, and resilience are at the heart of this endeavor. You'll learn how to tailor meals to your preferences, scale recipes to suit your requirements, and utilize seasonal produce to bring variety and vibrancy to your table. This book also highlights the importance of mindfulness and moderation, encouraging you to enjoy your meals fully and listen to your body's cues.

Physical activity, too, plays an integral part in this lifestyle. Integrating regular physical activity into your routine enhances the diet's benefits, contributing to an extensive approach to health. And as you explore this path, remember that you're not alone. Building a supportive network, whether through family, friends, or online connections, can give you the motivation and inspiration you require to remain consistent with your new eating habits.

This book also explains how you can adapt meal prepping to life changing situations, discussing the natural ebb and flow of life. It addresses how to stay true to your dietary notions in the face of unforeseen circumstances. Whether it's a change in your work schedule, a family gathering, or simply a shift in season, this book offers recommendations for adhering to the Atlantic Diet's key principles.

As you turn these pages, you'll be taken on an adventure that goes beyond the traditional concept of dieting. It's a journey of discovery, wellness, and culinary adventure. It's about nourishing your body with healthy meals, relishing the process of cooking, and savoring the numerous flavors of the Atlantic coast. Allow this book to function as a guide, inspiration, and companion on your path to a better, happier version of yourself.

UNLOCK YOUR EXCLUSIVE BONUSES HERE!

In appreciation for choosing this book, we are thrilled to offer you complimentary access to four essential meal planning tools designed to elevate your cooking experience. To gain access, simply scan this QR code!

CHAPTER 1: FOUNDATIONS OF ATLANTIC DIET MEAL PREP

The Atlantic Diet and Meal Prep Essentials

The Atlantic Diet and meal prepping serves as the cornerstone of your journey into the world of healthy, sustainable eating, inspired by the coastal regions surrounding the Atlantic Ocean. This establishes the foundation for a lifestyle that combines the rich cooking practices of Northern Portugal and Galicia in Spain with the modern practice of meal prepping, offering an enjoyable and attainable road to wellness.

The Atlantic Diet is centered on the abundant resources of the Atlantic Ocean and its surrounding lands. Central to this diet are fresh fish and seafood, which provide a wealth of omega-3 fatty acids, essential for heart health and cognitive function. Complementing these are a variety of fresh fruits and vegetables, whole grains, legumes, and nuts, all drizzled with the golden goodness of olive oil. Dairy products are typically consumed in moderation, and red meat is only used on occasion to ensure that meals are balanced and nourishing.

Transitioning to the Atlantic Diet through meal planning provides a unique set of benefits. Meal prepping not only saves time and stress, but also guarantees that you have healthy, diet-compliant meals accessible throughout the week. This method is especially beneficial for people with busy schedules who might otherwise choose less healthy eating options.

Essentials for Successful Meal Prepping on the Atlantic Diet

Understanding the Diet's Core Components: Knowledge of the Atlantic Diet's fundamental ingredients is important. Emphasis is on seasonal and locally sourced produce, fish, and whole grains. This guarantees that your meal preps are not only nutritious, but also conform to the diet's principles.

Strategic Planning: Start with a weekly meal plan that includes a variety of meals to attain nutritional balance and prevent boredom. Consider the seasonality of ingredients to ensure maximum freshness and flavor.

Efficient Shopping: Compile a shopping list based on your meal plan. To streamline your shopping experience, organize your list by food categories. To reduce cost and avoid packaging waste, buy in bulk whenever feasible.

Preparation and Storage: Allocate a few hours each week to prepare and cook your meals in batches. Invest in high-quality storage containers to keep your meals fresh and make portion management easier. Labeling containers with contents and dates can help you keep track of your meals.

Adaptability: Be prepared to modify recipes based on available ingredients. The Atlantic Diet is adaptable, allowing for variations that can keep your meal preparations exciting and diverse.

Key Tools and Equipment

Quality Knives: Essential for efficiently prepping vegetables, fish, and other ingredients.

Cookware: A collection of pots, pans, and baking dishes suited for preparing a wide range of dishes.

Storage Containers: Durable, airtight containers for storing prepped meals in the fridge or freezer.

Blender or food processor: Ideal for making sauces, dressings, and smoothies.

The Benefits of Meal Prepping

Meal prepping, the practice of planning and preparing meals in advance, offers a multitude of benefits that cater to one's health, time management, and financial savings.

Healthier Eating Habits: One of the most significant benefits of meal prepping is the fostering of healthier eating habits. When meals are planned and prepared in advance, there's a greater likelihood of making nutritious choices. The Atlantic Diet, with its emphasis on fish and seafood, fresh fruits and vegetables, whole grains, and healthy fats, provides an excellent nutritional foundation. Meal prepping ensures that each meal adheres to these guidelines, aiding in maintaining a balanced diet, regulating portion sizes, and reducing the temptation to choose unhealthy convenience food items.

Time Efficiency and Reduced Stress: Meal prepping saves time in the long run. Dedicating a few hours to prepare meals for the week means less time spent cooking and cleaning up daily. This efficiency is especially useful for people who have busy schedules. Knowing that your meals are ready and waiting for you can considerably reduce the stress and mental strain associated with daily meal planning and preparation.

Cost-Effective: Planning and preparing meals in advance can lead to financial savings. Buying ingredients in bulk, reducing impulse purchases, and minimizing food waste are all economical benefits of meal prepping. Additionally, when you have prepared meals ready to go, you're less likely to spend money on takeout or restaurant dining, which can be more expensive and less healthy.

Consistent Diet Adherence: For those following specific dietary guidelines, like the Atlantic Diet, meal prepping ensures consistency in complying with your dietary goals. It helps in maintaining a steady intake of the diverse nutrients the diet offers, which is crucial for a healthier lifestyle.

Enhanced Flavor and Variety: Meal prepping doesn't mean eating the same thing every day. It encourages creativity and variety in your diet. You can prepare different dishes that align with the Atlantic Diet, ensuring a range of flavors and textures throughout the week. This variety keeps meals interesting and enjoyable, which is key to sustaining any dietary lifestyle.

Better Portion Control: Preparing your meals in advance allows for precise control over portion sizes, which is important for those monitoring their intake for weight management or specific health reasons. It also helps in recognizing and responding to your body's hunger and fullness indicators, resulting in an appropriate relationship with food.

Environmental Impact: Meal prepping can contribute to a reduced environmental footprint. By planning and cooking in batches, you can decrease energy usage compared to cooking meals individually. Moreover, meal prepping often leads to less food waste, as you only buy and prepare what you need.

Stocking Your Pantry for Success

This is a critical component that establishes the basis for efficient and effective meal planning within the Atlantic Diet paradigm. A well-stocked pantry is the foundation of any effective meal prep routine, ensuring that you have all of the goods on hand to prepare nutritious and tasty meals that adhere to the Atlantic Diet's principles.

The Essentials of a Well-Stocked Pantry

1. **Whole Grains and Legumes:** The Atlantic Diet is built on a foundation of whole grains such as quinoa, brown rice, barley, and oats, as well as legumes like lentils, chickpeas, and beans. These essentials not only supply important nutrients and fiber, but they also provide an excellent foundation for a plethora of recipes.
2. **Healthy Fats:** The Atlantic Diet favors olive oil, which is high in heart-healthy monounsaturated fats. Stockpiling high-quality extra virgin olive oil is critical for dressings, sautés, and drizzling on finished meals. Nuts and seeds, such as almonds, walnuts, chia, and flaxseeds, are excellent sources of healthy fats and can add texture and nutrition to dishes.
3. **Herbs and Spices:** Fresh and dried herbs, along with a selection of spices, are essential for infusing meals with flavor without the need for excessive salt or fat. Garlic, onions, paprika, saffron, and parsley constitute key ingredients in many Atlantic Diet recipes. These not only enhance taste and flavor but also provide a variety of health benefits.

4. **Canned and Jarred Goods:** Having a selection of canned fish, such as sardines, mackerel, and tuna, in your pantry ensures that you always have a quick protein option. Choose fish packed in olive oil or water for the healthiest options. Canned tomatoes, artichokes, and roasted red peppers also provide convenient, healthy alternatives for adding depth to dishes.
5. **Vinegars and Condiments:** Vinegars such as red wine, balsamic, and apple cider are excellent choices for creating dressings and adding acidity to dishes. Mustard, capers, and olives can add bold flavors to your meals, corresponding with the Atlantic Diet's preference for vibrant, natural tastes.

Organizing your pantry

An organized pantry is just as important as a well-stocked one. Group items by category and use clear, labeled containers for bulk items like grains and legumes. This not only makes items easy to find, but it also helps to keep them fresh and monitor what needs to be restocked.

Sustainable and Seasonal Choices

When stocking your pantry, think about the sustainability of the products you buy. Opt for local and seasonal items when possible, and look for certifications that indicate sustainable practices, especially for seafood. This approach not only supports the principles of the Atlantic Diet but also contributes to a healthier planet.

Pantry's Role in Meal Prep

A thoughtfully stocked pantry simplifies the meal prep process, allowing for creativity and flexibility in your weekly meal planning. With the essentials on hand, you can easily assemble nutritious meals, even on your busiest days. The pantry acts as your culinary toolbox, allowing you to create meals that are not only healthy and nutritious, but also diverse and enjoyable, ensuring a long-term adherence to this wholesome way of eating.

CHAPTER 2: MEAL PREP STARTEGIES

Setting Up Your Meal Prep Routine

Setting your prepping routine is an important aspect that guides you through the process of creating a disciplined approach to meal planning within the context of the Atlantic Diet. This practice is intended to streamline your cooking process, allowing you to enjoy nutritious, tasty meals even on your busiest days.

The first step in developing your meal prep routine is to set out a certain day and time each week for meal planning and preparation. Sunday is a popular choice for many, as it allows you to prepare meals for the upcoming week. However, choose a day that best fits your schedule.

Understanding Your Dietary Needs: Before starting your meal prepping, assess your dietary requirements. The Atlantic Diet focuses on fish and seafood, whole grains, fresh fruits, and vegetables. Consider any personal or family dietary needs, preferences, and any goals you might have, such as weight management or addressing specific health issues.

Planning Your Meals: Start with a weekly meal plan that includes a variety of dishes for breakfast, lunch, and dinner, making sure each meal aligns with the Atlantic Diet's principles. Planning includes deciding which meals will be cooked fresh and which ones will be prepped in advance. Incorporate flexibility in your meal plan for days when you might prefer to cook fresh fish or seafood, taking advantage of their optimal freshness.

Shopping Smart: With your meal plan in hand, create a detailed shopping list. To make your shopping trip more efficient, organize your list by department (produce, seafood, and pantry items). Focus on buying seasonal and local produce to bring out the flavors of your meals while supporting local communities. When choosing fish and seafood, seek out sustainable sources to guarantee environmental responsibility.

Prepping Ingredients: Wash, chop, and portion out your fruits and vegetables as soon as you get home from the market. Pre-cooking grains and legumes can help save a lot of time during the week. Fish and seafood require appropriate storage. Fresh seafood should be cooked within a day or two, and some can be portioned and stored for later use.

Batch cooking and portioning involve preparing and cooking meals in batches. This could mean roasting a large batch of vegetables, grilling several pieces of fish, or making a big pot of soup. Once cooked, portion your meals into individual containers. Consider the best means of preserving freshness, such as refrigerating meals that will be eaten within a few days and freezing others for later in the week.

Labeling and Organizing: Label your containers with the contents and the date prepared. This not only helps you quickly identify what you need but also ensures you use the oldest meals first, reducing waste.

Adaptability and Flexibility: Your meal prep approach should be adaptable to changes in your schedule, ingredient availability, and dietary choices. Be willing to substitute items in recipes based on what's fresh and accessible. This adaptability is key to maintaining a sustainable meal prep routine.

By establishing a solid meal prep routine, you're not just organizing your meals for the week; you're setting yourself up for success in adhering to the Atlantic Diet. This practice serves as the foundation for a lifestyle that emphasizes the richness of Atlantic coastal meals, making it easier to bring healthy, delectable meals to your table.

Creating a Balanced Meal Plan

Creating a balanced meal plan is important in meal prepping because it guides you on how to construct a meal plan that not only conforms to the principles of dieting but also ensures a well-rounded nutritional intake. This approach entails careful assessment of macronutrients, micronutrients, and overall caloric balance, tailored to individual health goals and lifestyle requirements.

Step-by-Step Guide to Balanced Meal Planning

1. **Diversify Protein Sources:** Include a variety of seafood in your weekly meal plan, such as salmon, mackerel, and sardines, as well as plant-based proteins like lentils and chickpeas. This variety guarantees a sufficient supply of essential amino acids and omega-3 fatty acids.
2. **Incorporate Whole Grains:** Choose whole grains such as oats, quinoa, and brown rice as the base for meals. These grains supply continuous energy, fiber, and essential B vitamins, aiding digestion and energy levels throughout the day.
3. **Emphasize Fruits and Vegetables:** Aim for a dynamic list of fruits and vegetables to ensure a broad spectrum of vitamins, minerals, and antioxidants. Each color represents different nutrients, so the more variety, the better.
4. **Include Healthy Fats:** Olive oil should be the primary fat source, used in cooking and dressings. Nuts and seeds can be utilized as snacks or garnishes, providing essential fatty acids and additional protein.
5. **Stay Hydrated:** While not a food group, hydration plays a significant role in overall health. Include reminders to drink water throughout the day, and consider herbal teas as a warming, antioxidant-rich beverage.

Practical Tips for Meal Planning

1. **Start Small:** If you are new to meal planning, start by planning a few days at a time to avoid becoming overwhelmed.
2. **Plan for Leftovers:** Cook once, eat twice. Many meals can be repurposed into new dishes the following day, saving time and reducing waste.
3. **Seasonal and Local:** Focus on seasonal produce and locally sourced seafood, ensuring freshness and supporting local economies.
4. **Flexibility is key:** Life is unpredictable. Design your meal plan with some flexibility to accommodate last-minute changes or cravings.
5. **Batch Cooking:** Prepare larger quantities of staples like grains and legumes, and store them for use throughout the week. This approach saves time and streamlines meal preparation.
6. **Snacks Count Too:** Include healthy snacks in your meal plan, such as fruit with nuts or yogurt, to maintain energy levels and prevent overeating at meal times.

Efficient Shopping Strategies

This strategy is crucial for those starting a meal prep journey based on the Atlantic Diet. This section offers practical suggestions on how to shop effectively, ensuring that your pantry and fridge are stocked with the necessary ingredients for a week of nutritious meals without overspending or wasting food.

Planning Ahead

A well-thought-out plan is required for productive shopping. Before heading to the shop, make a list of what you already have in your kitchen to avoid purchasing duplicates. Create an extensive shopping list based on your meal plan, categorizing things by department (produce, seafood, dairy, etc.) to help you streamline your shopping trip. This not only saves time, but also helps you resist impulse purchases that do not align with the Atlantic Diet.

Embracing Seasonality and Locality

Focusing on seasonal and local produce is not only environmentally sustainable but often more affordable and flavorful. Seasonal fruits and vegetables are at their peak, meaning they're packed with nutrients and taste. Additionally, purchasing local seafood guarantees freshness and supports the local economy. Familiarize yourself with the seasonal produce in your area and build your meal plan around these items.

Buying in Bulk

For non-perishable items such as whole grains, legumes, and nuts, consider buying in bulk. Bulk purchases are typically cost-effective and reduce packaging waste. To avoid waste, take into account storage space and shelf life. Investing in airtight containers can help keep bulk items fresh for longer.

Understanding Sales and Discounts

Keep an eye on sales and discounts, especially for more expensive items like seafood. Numerous stores provide discounts on certain days of the week or have loyalty programs that offer savings. Be flexible in your meal plan to integrate sale items, substituting one type of fish or vegetable for another based on what's on offer.

Prioritizing Quality and Sustainability

When it comes to seafood, quality and sustainability are paramount. Look for certifications such as Marine Stewardship Council (MSC) or Aquaculture Stewardship Council (ASC) to guarantee that you are purchasing responsibly sourced seafood. While these options might be pricier, they're better for the environment and often taste superior. Remember, the Atlantic Diet emphasizes the quality of ingredients, so this is an area worth investing in.

Minimizing Waste

Efficient shopping also involves minimizing food waste. Plan to use perishable items like fresh herbs and vegetables early in the week, and save longer-lasting ingredients for subsequent meals. Consider how you can repurpose leftovers into new meals, turning last night's grilled fish into today's salad topping, for example.

Online Shopping and Delivery Services

For individuals with busy schedules, online shopping and delivery services can be a game changer. Many services allow you to save shopping lists, making it easy to reorder staples. Just be sure to thoroughly evaluate items to verify they are consistent with your meal plan and nutritional goals.

Time-Saving Cooking Techniques

Time-saving cooking techniques are a necessity for individuals who want to effectively incorporate the Atlantic Diet into their busy lives. This section focuses on practical strategies for reducing cooking time, making it easier to create nutritious, enjoyable meals that follow the Atlantic Diet principles. These strategies not only simplify the cooking process, but also ensure that meal preparation becomes a sustainable part of your weekly routines.

Batch cooking

One of the most effective time-saving techniques is batch cooking. This involves preparing large quantities of certain dishes or components at once, such as grains, legumes, roasted vegetables, or poached fish. These can then be stored in the refrigerator or freezer and used as the base for various meals throughout the week. For example, a big batch of quinoa can serve as a side dish, a salad base, or a breakfast porridge ingredient.

One-Pot Meals

One-pot or one-pan meals are beneficial for time-saving cooking. These recipes minimize cleanup and often involve simmering ingredients together, allowing flavors to meld while requiring minimal active cooking time. Think in terms of satisfying stews, seafood paellas, or sheet-pan roasted fish with a medley of seasonal vegetables. These recipes capture the spirit of the Atlantic Diet and can be made in large portions for multiple meals.

Utilizing a Pressure Cooker or Slow Cooker

Pressure cookers and slow cookers are excellent tools for preparing meals in advance with minimal effort. A slow cooker can simmer a fish stew or soup throughout the day, ready for dinner with little to no active supervision. A pressure cooker can significantly reduce the cooking time of whole grains and legumes, which are staples of the Atlantic Diet, making them more accessible for weeknight dinners.

Pre-Cut or Frozen Vegetables

While fresh produce is an essential component of the Atlantic Diet, there is nothing wrong with utilizing pre-cut or frozen vegetables to save time. These options are particularly useful for labor-intensive vegetables or when you're short on prep time. Frozen vegetables are picked and frozen at their peak freshness, retaining their nutritional value and flavor.

High-Heat Cooking Methods

Techniques like broiling, grilling, and stir-frying can cook foods quickly while adding a delicious char or crispness. For example, fish fillets can be broiled in just a few minutes, offering a speedy way to prepare a protein-rich, Atlantic Diet-friendly centerpiece for your meal. Similarly, stir-frying allows you to quickly cook vegetables, maintaining their crunch and nutritional content.

Prepping Ingredients in Advance

A little advanced planning can go a long way. Washing and chopping vegetables, portioning out spices, or marinating fish ahead of time can make the actual cooking process much more efficient. Having these items ready to go means you can assemble and cook meals with minimal delay.

Simplifying Recipes

Not every meal needs to be a gourmet affair. Simplifying recipes to focus on the quality and flavors of a few key ingredients can reduce cooking time without sacrificing taste or nutritional value. This is entirely consistent with the Atlantic Diet's emphasis on fresh, high-quality products prepared straightforwardly.

Implementing these time-saving cooking techniques into your meal prep routine can transform the process from a time-consuming chore to a fun, achievable part of the week. By streamlining meal preparation, the Atlantic Diet becomes not just a nutritional guideline but a feasible lifestyle choice, even for those with the busiest of schedules.

CHAPTER 3: BREAKFAST RECIPES

Smoked Salmon Avocado Toast

Preparation Time: 10 minutes
Cook Time: 0 minutes
Number of Serves: 2

Ingredients:

- 4 slices whole-grain bread
- 1 ripe avocado
- 4 ounces smoked salmon
- 1 tablespoon lemon juice
- Salt and pepper to taste
- Fresh dill for garnish
- Red onion slices (optional)

Instructions:

1. Toast the whole-grain bread slices to your preference.
2. Mash the avocado in a bowl and mix in the lemon juice, salt, and pepper.
3. Spread the mashed avocado evenly over the toasted bread.
4. Top each slice with smoked salmon, a sprinkle of fresh dill, and red onion slices if desired.
5. Serve immediately.

Nutritional Information (per serving):

- Calories: 300
- Protein: 15g
- Carbohydrates: 30g
- Fat: 15g
- Fiber: 7g

Seafood Frittata

Preparation Time: 15 minutes
Cook Time: 25 minutes
Number of Serves: 4

Ingredients:

- 6 large eggs
- 1/4 cup milk
- 1 cup mixed seafood (shrimp, crab, scallops), cooked
- 1/2 cup cherry tomatoes, halved
- 1/4 cup feta cheese, crumbled
- 2 tablespoons fresh parsley, chopped
- Salt and pepper to taste
- 1 tablespoon olive oil

Instructions:

1. Preheat your oven to 375°F (190°C).
2. In a large mixing bowl, whisk together eggs, milk, salt, and pepper.
3. Stir in the cooked seafood, cherry tomatoes, feta cheese, and parsley.
4. Heat olive oil in an oven-safe skillet over medium heat. Pour in the egg mixture.
5. Cook for 5 minutes until the edges begin to set.
6. Transfer the skillet to the oven and bake for 20 minutes, or until the frittata is set and lightly golden.
7. Let cool for a few minutes before slicing and serving.

Nutritional Information (per serving):

- Calories: 220
- Protein: 20g
- Carbohydrates: 4g
- Fat: 14g
- Fiber: 1g

Quinoa Berry Breakfast Bowl

Preparation Time: 5 minutes (plus overnight soaking if using uncooked quinoa)
Cook Time: 15 minutes (if cooking quinoa)
Number of Serves: 2

Ingredients:

- 1 cup cooked quinoa
- 1/2 cup mixed berries (strawberries, blueberries, raspberries)
- 1/4 cup Greek yogurt
- 2 tablespoons chopped nuts (almonds, walnuts)
- 1 tablespoon honey or maple syrup
- A pinch of cinnamon (optional)

Instructions:

1. If starting with uncooked quinoa, rinse 1/2 cup of quinoa under cold water, then cook according to package instructions. Allow to cool.
2. Divide the cooked quinoa between two bowls.
3. Top each bowl with mixed berries, a dollop of Greek yogurt, and chopped nuts.
4. Drizzle with honey or maple syrup and sprinkle with cinnamon if desired.
5. Serve immediately or refrigerate overnight for a chilled breakfast bowl.

Nutritional Information (per serving):

- Calories: 280
- Protein: 10g
- Carbohydrates: 45g
- Fat: 8g
- Fiber: 5g

Sardine and Tomato on Wholegrain

Preparation Time: 10 minutes
Cook Time: 0 minutes
Number of Serves: 2

Ingredients:

- 4 slices whole-grain bread
- 1 can sardines in olive oil, drained
- 1 large tomato, sliced
- Salt and pepper to taste
- Fresh basil leaves for garnish

Instructions:

1. Toast the whole-grain bread slices until golden and crispy.
2. Arrange the sardine fillets on the toasted bread slices.
3. Top each slice with fresh tomato slices. Season with salt and pepper.
4. Garnish with fresh basil leaves before serving.

Nutritional Information (per serving):

- Calories: 250
- Protein: 15g
- Carbohydrates: 28g
- Fat: 9g
- Fiber: 5g

Mackerel and Sweet Potato Hash

Preparation Time: 15 minutes
Cook Time: 20 minutes
Number of Serves: 4

Ingredients:

- 2 large sweet potatoes, peeled and diced
- 1 onion, diced
- 2 tablespoons olive oil
- 1 can mackerel in olive oil, drained and flaked
- Salt and pepper to taste
- 2 tablespoons fresh parsley, chopped

Instructions:

1. Heat the olive oil in a large skillet over medium heat. Add the diced sweet potatoes and onion. Cook until the sweet potatoes are tender and the onion is translucent, about 15 minutes, stirring occasionally.
2. Add the flaked mackerel to the skillet. Stir to combine and cook until heated through, about 5 minutes.
3. Season with salt and pepper to taste. Garnish with fresh parsley before serving.

Nutritional Information (per serving):

- Calories: 320
- Protein: 15g
- Carbohydrates: 38g
- Fat: 14g
- Fiber: 6g

Oatmeal with Poached Pear

Preparation Time: 10 minutes
Cook Time: 20 minutes
Number of Serves: 2

Ingredients:

- 1 cup rolled oats
- 2 cups water or milk
- 1 pear, halved and cored
- 1 cinnamon stick
- 2 tablespoons honey or maple syrup
- 1/4 cup chopped nuts (walnuts, almonds)

Instructions:

1. In a saucepan, bring the water or milk to a boil. Add the rolled oats and reduce the heat to simmer. Cook, stirring occasionally, until the oats are soft and creamy, about 10 minutes.
2. In another saucepan, add enough water to cover the pear halves. Add the cinnamon stick and bring to a simmer. Place the pear halves in the simmering water and poach until tender, about 10 minutes.
3. Divide the cooked oatmeal between two bowls. Place a poached pear half in each bowl.
4. Drizzle with honey or maple syrup and sprinkle with chopped nuts before serving.

Nutritional Information (per serving):

- Calories: 350
- Protein: 8g
- Carbohydrates: 60g
- Fat: 10g
- Fiber: 8g

Berry Chia Pudding

Preparation Time: 10 minutes (plus overnight for setting)
Cook Time: 0 minutes
Number of Serves: 2

Ingredients:

- 1/4 cup chia seeds
- 1 cup almond milk (or any plant-based milk)
- 1 tablespoon honey or maple syrup
- 1/2 teaspoon vanilla extract
- 1/2 cup mixed berries (fresh or frozen)

Instructions:

1. In a bowl, mix the chia seeds, almond milk, honey (or maple syrup), and vanilla extract until well combined.
2. Cover the bowl and refrigerate overnight, or until the chia seeds have absorbed the liquid and the mixture has a pudding-like consistency.
3. Serve the chia pudding in bowls or glasses, topped with mixed berries.

Nutritional Information (per serving):

- Calories: 200
- Protein: 5g
- Carbohydrates: 24g
- Fat: 10g
- Fiber: 10g

Greek Yogurt with Honeyed Walnuts

Preparation Time: 5 minutes
Cook Time: 5 minutes (for walnuts)
Number of Serves: 2

Ingredients:

- 1 cup Greek yogurt
- 1/4 cup walnuts, roughly chopped
- 2 tablespoons honey
- A pinch of cinnamon (optional)

Instructions:

1. In a small pan, toast the chopped walnuts over medium heat for about 2-3 minutes until fragrant. Be careful not to burn them.
2. Drizzle the honey over the toasted walnuts in the pan, stirring quickly to coat. Allow to cool slightly.
3. Serve the Greek yogurt in bowls, topped with the honeyed walnuts. Sprinkle a pinch of cinnamon on top if desired.

Nutritional Information (per serving):

- Calories: 220
- Protein: 12g
- Carbohydrates: 18g
- Fat: 12g
- Fiber: 1g

Spinach and Feta Scrambled Eggs

Preparation Time: 5 minutes
Cook Time: 10 minutes
Number of Serves: 2

Ingredients:

- 4 large eggs
- 1/4 cup milk
- 1/2 cup fresh spinach, chopped
- 1/4 cup feta cheese, crumbled
- Salt and pepper to taste
- 1 tablespoon olive oil

Instructions:

1. In a bowl, whisk together the eggs, milk, salt, and pepper until well combined.
2. Heat the olive oil in a non-stick skillet over medium heat.
3. Add the chopped spinach to the skillet and sauté for 1-2 minutes until slightly wilted.
4. Pour the egg mixture into the skillet with the spinach. Allow it to set for a few seconds, then gently scramble the eggs with a spatula, pushing from the edges towards the center.
5. When the eggs are almost set but still slightly runny, sprinkle the crumbled feta cheese over the top. Continue to cook for another minute until the eggs are fully set and the feta is slightly melted.
6. Serve immediately, optionally with a side of whole-grain toast.

Nutritional Information (per serving):

- Calories: 250
- Protein: 18g
- Carbohydrates: 3g
- Fat: 19g
- Fiber: 0.5g

Shrimp and Avocado Salad

Preparation Time: 15 minutes
Cook Time: 5 minutes
Number of Serves: 2

Ingredients:

- 8 ounces shrimp, peeled and deveined
- 1 ripe avocado, diced
- 2 cups mixed salad greens (e.g., arugula, spinach, romaine)
- 1/2 cup cherry tomatoes, halved
- 1/4 cup cucumber, sliced
- 2 tablespoons olive oil, divided
- 1 tablespoon lemon juice
- Salt and pepper to taste
- 1 tablespoon fresh cilantro, chopped (optional)

Instructions:

1. Heat 1 tablespoon of olive oil in a skillet over medium-high heat. Add the shrimp, season with salt and pepper, and cook for 2-3 minutes on each side or until they are pink and opaque. Remove from heat and let cool.
2. In a large bowl, combine the mixed salad greens, cherry tomatoes, cucumber, and diced avocado.
3. In a small bowl, whisk together the remaining olive oil, lemon juice, salt, and pepper to create the dressing.
4. Add the cooled shrimp to the salad, pour over the dressing, and gently toss to combine. Garnish with chopped cilantro if desired.
5. Serve immediately.

Nutritional Information (per serving):

- Calories: 320
- Protein: 24g
- Carbohydrates: 12g
- Fat: 20g
- Fiber: 6g

CHAPTER 4: LUNCH RECIPES

Tuna Niçoise Salad

Preparation Time: 20 minutes
Cook Time: 10 minutes
Number of Serves: 4

Ingredients:
- 4 fresh tuna steaks (about 6 ounces each)
- 8 small new potatoes, halved
- 4 eggs
- 2 cups green beans, trimmed
- 1 cup cherry tomatoes, halved
- 1/2 cup black olives, pitted
- Mixed salad greens

For the dressing:
- 3 tablespoons olive oil
- 1 tablespoon red wine vinegar
- 1 teaspoon Dijon mustard
- Salt and pepper to taste

Instructions:
1. Boil the potatoes until tender, about 10 minutes. Drain and set aside to cool.
2. In the same pot, boil the eggs to your desired doneness, about 7 minutes for hard-boiled. Cool, peel, and quarter the eggs.
3. Blanch the green beans in boiling water for 2-3 minutes, then plunge into ice water to stop the cooking process. Drain.
4. Grill or pan-sear the tuna steaks over high heat to your preferred doneness, about 2-3 minutes per side for medium-rare.
5. Whisk together the ingredients for the dressing in a small bowl.
6. Assemble the salad by arranging the greens, potatoes, green beans, tomatoes, and olives on a plate. Top with the tuna steak and quartered eggs.
7. Drizzle with the dressing just before serving.

Nutritional Information (per serving):
- Calories: 400
- Protein: 40g
- Carbohydrates: 20g
- Fat: 18g
- Fiber: 5g

Simple Seafood Paella

Preparation Time: 15 minutes
Cook Time: 40 minutes
Number of Serves: 4

Ingredients:
- 2 tablespoons olive oil
- 1 onion, finely chopped
- 2 garlic cloves, minced
- 1 cup Arborio rice
- 1/2 teaspoon saffron threads
- 4 cups fish or chicken broth
- 1 cup diced tomatoes
- 1 cup green peas
- 1 pound mixed seafood (shrimp, mussels, and squid rings)
- Salt and pepper to taste
- Lemon wedges for serving

Instructions:
1. Heat the olive oil in a large skillet or paella pan over medium heat. Add the onion and garlic, and sauté until soft.
2. Stir in the rice and saffron, coating the rice in the oil and toasting it lightly.
3. Add the broth and diced tomatoes, bringing the mixture to a simmer. Cook, uncovered, for about 20 minutes, stirring occasionally.
4. Add the green peas and mixed seafood, nestling them into the rice. Cover and cook for an additional 10-15 minutes, or until the seafood is cooked through and the rice is tender.
5. Season with salt and pepper to taste. Serve hot with lemon wedges on the side.

Nutritional Information (per serving):
- Calories: 450
- Protein: 30g
- Carbohydrates: 60g
- Fat: 10g
- Fiber: 4g

Salmon and Quinoa Salad

Preparation Time: 15 minutes
Cook Time: 20 minutes
Number of Serves: 4

Ingredients:
- 4 salmon fillets (about 6 ounces each)
- 1 cup quinoa
- 2 cups water
- 1 avocado, diced
- 1 cup cherry tomatoes, halved
- 1/2 cucumber, diced
- 1/4 cup red onion, finely chopped
- 1/4 cup fresh cilantro, chopped
  - *For the dressing:*
    - 3 tablespoons lime juice
    - 2 tablespoons olive oil
    - 1 teaspoon honey
    - Salt and pepper to taste

Instructions:
1. Rinse the quinoa under cold water. In a pot, bring the quinoa and water to a boil. Reduce heat, cover, and simmer until the quinoa is tender and the water is absorbed, about 15 minutes. Fluff with a fork and let cool.
2. Grill or pan-sear the salmon to your preferred doneness, about 4-5 minutes per side for medium.
3. In a large bowl, combine the cooled quinoa, avocado, cherry tomatoes, cucumber, red onion, and cilantro.
4. Whisk together the lime juice, olive oil, honey, salt, and pepper to make the dressing.
5. Flake the cooked salmon and gently fold it into the quinoa salad.
6. Drizzle the dressing over the salad, toss gently to combine, and serve immediately.

Nutritional Information (per serving):
- Calories: 450
- Protein: 35g
- Carbohydrates: 40g
- Fat: 18g
- Fiber: 6g

Portuguese Fish Stew

Preparation Time: 15 minutes
Cook Time: 30 minutes
Number of Serves: 4

Ingredients:
- 2 tablespoons olive oil
- 1 onion, chopped
- 2 garlic cloves, minced
- 1 bell pepper, chopped
- 2 potatoes, cubed
- 1 can (14 oz) diced tomatoes
- 4 cups fish stock
- 1 teaspoon paprika
- 1 bay leaf
- 1 pound firm white fish (e.g., cod, haddock), cut into chunks
- Salt and pepper to taste
- Chopped parsley for garnish

Instructions:
1. Heat the olive oil in a large pot over medium heat. Add the onion, garlic, and bell pepper, sautéing until softened.
2. Add the potatoes, diced tomatoes, fish stock, paprika, and bay leaf. Bring to a simmer and cook until the potatoes are tender, about 20 minutes.
3. Add the fish chunks to the pot, season with salt and pepper, and simmer gently until the fish is cooked through, about 10 minutes.
4. Remove the bay leaf, adjust seasoning if needed, and serve hot, garnished with chopped parsley.

Nutritional Information (per serving):
- Calories: 300
- Protein: 25g
- Carbohydrates: 30g
- Fat: 10g
- Fiber: 5g

Crab and Avocado Wrap

Preparation Time: 10 minutes
Cook Time: 0 minutes
Number of Serves: 2

Ingredients:

- 2 whole-grain wraps
- 6 ounces crab meat, cooked and chilled
- 1 avocado, sliced
- 1/2 cup mixed salad greens
- 1/4 cup diced tomato
- 2 tablespoons low-fat Greek yogurt
- 1 tablespoon lime juice
- Salt and pepper to taste

Instructions:

1. Lay out the whole-grain wraps on a flat surface.
2. In a small bowl, mix the crab meat with Greek yogurt, lime juice, salt, and pepper.
3. Divide the crab mixture evenly between the wraps, spreading it down the center.
4. Top with avocado slices, mixed salad greens, and diced tomato.
5. Roll up the wraps tightly, cut in half, and serve immediately.

Nutritional Information (per serving):

- Calories: 350
- Protein: 20g
- Carbohydrates: 35g
- Fat: 15g
- Fiber: 8g

Lentil Salad with Cod

Preparation Time: 15 minutes
Cook Time: 25 minutes
Number of Serves: 4

Ingredients:
- 1 cup green lentils
- 4 cod fillets (about 6 ounces each)
- 2 tablespoons olive oil
- 1 lemon, zest and juice
- 1 cup cherry tomatoes, halved
- 1/2 cucumber, diced
- 1/4 red onion, thinly sliced
- 1/4 cup fresh parsley, chopped
- Salt and pepper to taste

Instructions:
1. Cook the lentils according to package instructions until tender. Drain and set aside to cool.
2. Season the cod fillets with salt, pepper, and lemon zest. Heat 1 tablespoon of olive oil in a skillet over medium heat and cook the cod until opaque and flaky, about 4-5 minutes per side.
3. In a large bowl, combine the cooked lentils, cherry tomatoes, cucumber, red onion, and parsley. Drizzle with the remaining olive oil and lemon juice, tossing to coat.
4. Serve the lentil salad with a piece of cod on top, seasoned with additional salt, pepper, and lemon juice if desired.

Nutritional Information (per serving):
- Calories: 350
- Protein: 30g
- Carbohydrates: 40g
- Fat: 8g
- Fiber: 10g

Shrimp Mango Ceviche

Preparation Time: 20 minutes (plus 2 hours for marinating)
Cook Time: 0 minutes
Number of Serves: 4

Ingredients:

- 1 pound raw shrimp, peeled and deveined, chopped
- 1 ripe mango, diced
- 1/2 red onion, finely chopped
- 1 jalapeño, seeded and minced
- Juice of 2 limes
- Juice of 1 lemon
- 1/4 cup fresh cilantro, chopped
- Salt to taste
- Avocado slices and tortilla chips for serving

Instructions:

1. In a bowl, combine the shrimp with lime and lemon juice. Ensure the shrimp is covered in juice. Cover and refrigerate for about 2 hours, or until the shrimp are opaque and "cooked" through the acidity.
2. Once the shrimp is ready, add the mango, red onion, jalapeño, and cilantro to the bowl. Mix gently to combine. Season with salt to taste.
3. Serve the ceviche chilled, garnished with avocado slices, and accompanied by tortilla chips.

Nutritional Information (per serving):

- Calories: 180
- Protein: 24g
- Carbohydrates: 15g
- Fat: 3g
- Fiber: 2g

Grilled Sardine Bruschetta

Preparation Time: 15 minutes
Cook Time: 10 minutes
Number of Serves: 4

Ingredients:

- 8 fresh sardines, cleaned and gutted
- 4 slices of whole-grain bread
- 2 cloves garlic, halved
- 2 tomatoes, diced
- 1 tablespoon olive oil, plus extra for brushing
- Salt and freshly ground black pepper
- Fresh parsley, chopped for garnish

Instructions:

1. Preheat your grill to medium-high heat. Brush the sardines with olive oil and season with salt and pepper.
2. Grill the sardines for 2-3 minutes on each side, until cooked through and slightly charred.
3. While the sardines are grilling, toast the whole-grain bread slices. Rub the toasted bread with the halved garlic cloves for added flavor.
4. In a bowl, toss the diced tomatoes with 1 tablespoon of olive oil, salt, and pepper.
5. Top each garlic-rubbed toast slice with the grilled sardines. Spoon the tomato mixture over the sardines and garnish with chopped parsley.
6. Serve immediately.

Nutritional Information (per serving):

- Calories: 250
- Protein: 20g
- Carbohydrates: 18g
- Fat: 12g
- Fiber: 3g

Mediterranean Tuna Pasta Salad

Preparation Time: 15 minutes
Cook Time: 10 minutes
Number of Serves: 4

Ingredients:
- 8 ounces whole-wheat pasta (e.g., fusilli or penne)
- 1 can (6 ounces) tuna in olive oil, drained
- 1/2 cup cherry tomatoes, halved
- 1/4 cup black olives, pitted and sliced
- 1/4 cup red onion, finely chopped
- 1/4 cup feta cheese, crumbled
- 2 tablespoons capers, drained

   For the dressing:
   - 3 tablespoons olive oil
   - 2 tablespoons red wine vinegar
   - 1 teaspoon dried oregano
   - Salt and pepper to taste

Instructions:
1. Cook the pasta according to package instructions until al dente. Drain and rinse under cold water to cool.
2. In a large bowl, combine the cooled pasta, tuna, cherry tomatoes, black olives, red onion, feta cheese, and capers.
3. In a small bowl, whisk together the olive oil, red wine vinegar, oregano, salt, and pepper to create the dressing.
4. Pour the dressing over the pasta salad and toss to evenly coat.
5. Chill the salad in the refrigerator for at least 30 minutes before serving to allow the flavors to meld.

Nutritional Information (per serving):
- Calories: 360
- Protein: 18g
- Carbohydrates: 42g
- Fat: 15g
- Fiber: 6g

Haddock in Parchment with Vegetables

Preparation Time: 15 minutes
Cook Time: 20 minutes
Number of Serves: 4

Ingredients:
- 4 haddock fillets (about 6 ounces each)
- 2 zucchinis, thinly sliced
- 2 carrots, peeled and thinly sliced
- 1 red bell pepper, thinly sliced
- 4 teaspoons olive oil
- 4 tablespoons lemon juice
- Salt and freshly ground black pepper to taste
- Fresh dill or parsley for garnish
- 4 large parchment paper sheets

Instructions:
1. Preheat your oven to 400°F (200°C).
2. Cut the vegetables into thin slices and set aside.
3. Place each haddock fillet on a sheet of parchment paper. Season both sides of the fillets with salt and pepper.
4. Divide the sliced vegetables evenly and place them on top of each fillet. Drizzle each with 1 teaspoon of olive oil and 1 tablespoon of lemon juice.
5. Fold the parchment paper over the fish and vegetables, twisting the ends to seal the packets.
6. Place the packets on a baking sheet and bake in the preheated oven for 20 minutes, or until the fish is cooked through and the vegetables are tender.
7. Carefully open the packets (watch out for the steam), and transfer the contents to plates. Garnish with fresh dill or parsley before serving.

Nutritional Information (per serving):
- Calories: 220
- Protein: 27g
- Carbohydrates: 8g
- Fat: 9g
- Fiber: 2g

CHAPTER 5: DINNER RECIPES

Baked Salmon with Roasted Veggies

Preparation Time: 15 minutes
Cook Time: 25 minutes
Number of Serves: 4

Ingredients:

- 4 salmon fillets (about 6 ounces each)
- 2 cups mixed vegetables (e.g., bell peppers, zucchini, cherry tomatoes, asparagus)
- 2 tablespoons olive oil
- 1 lemon, sliced
- Salt and freshly ground black pepper to taste
- Fresh herbs (e.g., dill, parsley) for garnish

Instructions:

1. Preheat your oven to 400°F (200°C). Line a baking sheet with parchment paper.
2. Toss the mixed vegetables with 1 tablespoon of olive oil, salt, and pepper. Spread them evenly on the prepared baking sheet and roast in the oven for 10 minutes.
3. Remove the baking sheet from the oven. Push the vegetables to the sides and place the salmon fillets in the center. Drizzle the remaining olive oil over the salmon and season with salt and pepper. Place lemon slices on top of each fillet.
4. Return the baking sheet to the oven and bake for an additional 12-15 minutes, or until the salmon is cooked through and the vegetables are tender and lightly caramelized.
5. Garnish with fresh herbs before serving.

Nutritional Information (per serving):

- Calories: 350
- Protein: 35g
- Carbohydrates: 10g
- Fat: 20g
- Fiber: 3g

Creamy Seafood Risotto

Preparation Time: 10 minutes
Cook Time: 30 minutes
Number of Serves: 4

Ingredients:
- 1 tablespoon olive oil
- 1 small onion, finely chopped
- 2 garlic cloves, minced
- 1 cup Arborio rice
- 1/2 cup white wine (optional)
- 4 cups seafood or vegetable broth, warmed
- 1 pound mixed seafood (e.g., shrimp, scallops, squid rings)
- 1/2 cup grated Parmesan cheese
- Salt and freshly ground black pepper to taste
- Fresh parsley, chopped for garnish

Instructions:
1. Heat the olive oil in a large pan over medium heat. Add the onion and garlic, sautéing until soft and translucent.
2. Stir in the Arborio rice, toasting it lightly until it becomes slightly translucent.
3. Deglaze the pan with white wine, if using, and allow it to absorb into the rice.
4. Gradually add the warmed broth, one ladle at a time, stirring constantly and allowing each addition to be absorbed before adding the next. Continue until the rice is al dente, about 18-20 minutes.
5. Stir in the mixed seafood, cooking until just done, about 3-5 minutes.
6. Remove from heat, stir in the grated Parmesan, and season with salt and pepper. Garnish with chopped parsley before serving.

Nutritional Information (per serving):
- Calories: 450
- Protein: 30g
- Carbohydrates: 50g
- Fat: 12g
- Fiber: 2g

Cod in Tomato Chickpea Sauce

Preparation Time: 10 minutes
Cook Time: 20 minutes
Number of Serves: 4

Ingredients:
- 4 cod fillets (about 6 ounces each)
- 2 tablespoons olive oil
- 1 onion, chopped
- 2 garlic cloves, minced
- 1 can (14 oz) chickpeas, drained and rinsed
- 1 can (14 oz) diced tomatoes
- 1 teaspoon smoked paprika
- Salt and freshly ground black pepper to taste
- Fresh parsley, chopped for garnish

Instructions:
1. Heat 1 tablespoon of olive oil in a large skillet over medium heat. Add the onion and garlic, cooking until soft.
2. Stir in the chickpeas, diced tomatoes, and smoked paprika. Season with salt and pepper. Simmer the sauce for 10 minutes, allowing the flavors to meld.
3. In another pan, heat the remaining olive oil over medium-high heat. Season the cod fillets with salt and pepper, and sear them for about 2 minutes on each side, or until golden.
4. Gently place the seared cod fillets into the tomato chickpea sauce, spooning some sauce over the top of the fish. Cover and simmer for another 5-7 minutes, or until the cod is cooked through and flaky.
5. Garnish with fresh parsley before serving.

Nutritional Information (per serving):
- Calories: 350
- Protein: 30g
- Carbohydrates: 25g
- Fat: 15g
- Fiber: 6g

Mussels in White Wine

Preparation Time: 15 minutes
Cook Time: 10 minutes
Number of Serves: 4

Ingredients:

- 2 pounds fresh mussels, cleaned and debearded
- 1 tablespoon olive oil
- 2 shallots, finely chopped
- 3 garlic cloves, minced
- 1 cup white wine
- 2 tablespoons fresh parsley, chopped
- Salt and pepper to taste
- Crusty bread for serving

Instructions:

1. In a large pot, heat the olive oil over medium heat. Add the shallots and garlic, and sauté until soft and fragrant.
2. Pour in the white wine and bring to a simmer.
3. Add the cleaned mussels to the pot, cover, and cook for about 5-7 minutes, or until the mussels have opened. Discard any mussels that do not open.
4. Season with salt and pepper, and sprinkle with fresh parsley.
5. Serve hot with crusty bread to soak up the broth.

Nutritional Information (per serving):

- Calories: 200
- Protein: 18g
- Carbohydrates: 10g
- Fat: 6g
- Fiber: 0g

Grilled Swordfish with Quinoa

Preparation Time: 20 minutes
Cook Time: 15 minutes
Number of Serves: 4

Ingredients:

- 4 swordfish steaks (about 6 ounces each)
- 2 tablespoons olive oil
- 1 lemon, zest and juice
- Salt and pepper to taste
- 1 cup quinoa
- 2 cups water or vegetable broth
- 1/4 cup fresh basil, chopped
- Cherry tomatoes for garnish

Instructions:

1. Rinse the quinoa under cold water. In a saucepan, bring the quinoa and water or broth to a boil. Reduce heat, cover, and simmer until the quinoa is tender and the liquid is absorbed, about 15 minutes. Fluff with a fork and stir in the chopped basil.
2. Preheat the grill to medium-high heat. Brush the swordfish steaks with olive oil, and season with lemon zest, salt, and pepper.
3. Grill the swordfish steaks for about 3-4 minutes on each side, or until they are cooked through and have nice grill marks.
4. Serve the grilled swordfish over a bed of basil quinoa, drizzled with lemon juice and garnished with cherry tomatoes.

Nutritional Information (per serving):

- Calories: 350
- Protein: 35g
- Carbohydrates: 25g
- Fat: 12g
- Fiber: 3g

Sea Bass with Olive Salsa

Preparation Time: 15 minutes
Cook Time: 12 minutes
Number of Serves: 4

Ingredients:
- 4 sea bass fillets (about 6 ounces each)
- 2 tablespoons olive oil
- Salt and pepper to taste

  For the Olive Salsa:
    - 1/2 cup pitted olives, chopped
    - 1/4 cup red onion, finely chopped
    - 1 tablespoon capers, rinsed
    - 2 tablespoons fresh parsley, chopped
    - 1 tablespoon lemon juice
    - 2 tablespoons extra virgin olive oil
    - Salt and pepper to taste

Instructions:
1. Preheat your oven to 400°F (200°C). Line a baking sheet with parchment paper.
2. Place the sea bass fillets on the prepared baking sheet. Brush with olive oil, and season with salt and pepper.
3. Bake in the preheated oven for about 10-12 minutes, or until the fish is cooked through and flakes easily with a fork.
4. While the fish is baking, prepare the olive salsa by mixing together the chopped olives, red onion, capers, parsley, lemon juice, and extra virgin olive oil in a bowl. Season with salt and pepper to taste.
5. Serve the baked sea bass topped with the olive salsa.

Nutritional Information (per serving):
- Calories: 280
- Protein: 28g
- Carbohydrates: 4g
- Fat: 16g
- Fiber: 1g

Shrimp Asparagus Stir-Fry

Preparation Time: 15 minutes
Cook Time: 10 minutes
Number of Serves: 4

Ingredients:

- 1 pound shrimp, peeled and deveined
- 1 bunch asparagus, trimmed and cut into 1-inch pieces
- 2 tablespoons olive oil
- 2 garlic cloves, minced
- 1 tablespoon soy sauce (or tamari for gluten-free option)
- 1 teaspoon sesame oil
- Salt and pepper to taste
- Sesame seeds for garnish

Instructions:

1. Heat 1 tablespoon olive oil in a large skillet or wok over medium-high heat. Add the asparagus and stir-fry until tender-crisp, about 4-5 minutes. Remove from the skillet and set aside.
2. In the same skillet, add the remaining olive oil and garlic. Sauté for 30 seconds, then add the shrimp. Cook until the shrimp turn pink and are cooked through, about 3-4 minutes.
3. Return the asparagus to the skillet. Add soy sauce and sesame oil, tossing to combine all ingredients. Season with salt and pepper to taste.
4. Serve hot, garnished with sesame seeds.

Nutritional Information (per serving):

- Calories: 220
- Protein: 24g
- Carbohydrates: 6g
- Fat: 12g
- Fiber: 2g

Clam and Kale Soup

Preparation Time: 20 minutes
Cook Time: 30 minutes
Number of Serves: 4

Ingredients:

- 2 tablespoons olive oil
- 1 onion, chopped
- 2 garlic cloves, minced
- 1 bunch kale, stems removed and leaves chopped
- 4 cups vegetable broth
- 2 pounds clams, cleaned
- 1 cup diced potatoes
- Salt and pepper to taste
- Fresh parsley for garnish

Instructions:

1. In a large pot, heat the olive oil over medium heat. Add the onion and garlic, and sauté until softened, about 5 minutes.
2. Add the kale and sauté until wilted, about 2-3 minutes.
3. Pour in the vegetable broth and bring to a simmer. Add the diced potatoes and cook until tender, about 15 minutes.
4. Add the clams to the pot, cover, and cook until the clams have opened, about 5-7 minutes. Discard any clams that do not open.
5. Season the soup with salt and pepper to taste. Serve hot, garnished with fresh parsley.

Nutritional Information (per serving):

- Calories: 250
- Protein: 18g
- Carbohydrates: 20g
- Fat: 10g
- Fiber: 3g

Octopus and Potato Salad

Preparation Time: 15 minutes (plus time for cooking octopus)
Cook Time: 45 minutes (for octopus and potatoes)
Number of Serves: 4

Ingredients:

- 1 pound cooked octopus, cut into bite-sized pieces
- 4 medium potatoes, boiled and sliced
- 1/4 cup olive oil
- 2 tablespoons red wine vinegar
- 1 small red onion, thinly sliced
- 2 tablespoons fresh parsley, chopped
- Salt and pepper to taste
- Paprika for garnish

Instructions:

1. If the octopus is not pre-cooked, boil it in salted water until tender, about 45-60 minutes. Cool, then cut into bite-sized pieces.
2. In a large bowl, combine the sliced potatoes and octopus.
3. In a small bowl, whisk together the olive oil, red wine vinegar, salt, and pepper to create a dressing.
4. Pour the dressing over the octopus and potatoes. Add the sliced red onion and chopped parsley, and toss gently to combine.
5. Chill the salad for at least 30 minutes before serving. Garnish with a sprinkle of paprika.

Nutritional Information (per serving):

- Calories: 320
- Protein: 25g
- Carbohydrates: 30g
- Fat: 12g
- Fiber: 4g

Herb-Crusted Hake

Preparation Time: 15 minutes
Cook Time: 20 minutes
Number of Serves: 4

Ingredients:

- 4 hake fillets (about 6 ounces each)
- 1/2 cup breadcrumbs
- 2 tablespoons fresh parsley, finely chopped
- 1 tablespoon fresh thyme leaves
- 2 garlic cloves, minced
- Zest of 1 lemon
- 2 tablespoons olive oil
- Salt and pepper to taste
- Lemon wedges for serving

Instructions:

1. Preheat your oven to 400°F (200°C). Line a baking sheet with parchment paper.
2. In a bowl, mix together the breadcrumbs, parsley, thyme, garlic, and lemon zest. Season with salt and pepper.
3. Brush each hake fillet with olive oil, then press the herb breadcrumb mixture onto the top of each fillet to form a crust.
4. Place the crusted fillets on the prepared baking sheet and bake in the preheated oven for about 15-20 minutes, or until the fish is cooked through and the crust is golden and crispy.
5. Serve the herb-crusted hake hot, accompanied by lemon wedges for added zest.

Nutritional Information (per serving):

- Calories: 280
- Protein: 26g
- Carbohydrates: 10g
- Fat: 15g
- Fiber: 1g

CHAPTER 6: SNACKS AND SIDES

Garlic Roasted Brussels Sprouts

Preparation Time: 10 minutes
Cook Time: 25 minutes
Number of Serves: 4

Ingredients:

- 1 pound Brussels sprouts, trimmed and halved
- 3 tablespoons olive oil
- 4 garlic cloves, minced
- Salt and pepper to taste

Instructions:

1. Preheat your oven to 400°F (200°C).
2. In a large bowl, toss the Brussels sprouts with olive oil, minced garlic, salt, and pepper until well coated.
3. Spread the Brussels sprouts in a single layer on a baking sheet.
4. Roast in the preheated oven for 25 minutes, or until tender and caramelized, stirring halfway through.
5. Serve warm.

Nutritional Information (per serving):

- Calories: 120
- Protein: 4g
- Carbohydrates: 10g
- Fat: 8g
- Fiber: 4g

Cucumber Seaweed Salad

Preparation Time: 15 minutes (plus soaking time for seaweed)
Cook Time: 0 minutes
Number of Serves: 4

Ingredients:

- 1 cup dried seaweed (wakame), rehydrated and drained
- 2 cucumbers, thinly sliced
- 2 tablespoons rice vinegar
- 1 tablespoon soy sauce
- 1 teaspoon sesame oil
- 1 teaspoon sugar
- Sesame seeds for garnish

Instructions:

1. Soak the dried seaweed in water according to package instructions, then drain and squeeze out excess water.
2. In a mixing bowl, combine the rehydrated seaweed and sliced cucumbers.
3. In a small bowl, whisk together rice vinegar, soy sauce, sesame oil, and sugar until the sugar dissolves.
4. Pour the dressing over the seaweed and cucumber mixture and toss to coat evenly.
5. Chill in the refrigerator for at least 30 minutes before serving. Garnish with sesame seeds.

Nutritional Information (per serving):

- Calories: 50
- Protein: 2g
- Carbohydrates: 8g
- Fat: 2g
- Fiber: 1g

Spicy Roasted Chickpeas

Preparation Time: 5 minutes
Cook Time: 30 minutes
Number of Serves: 4

Ingredients:

- 2 cans (15 ounces each) chickpeas, drained, rinsed, and patted dry
- 2 tablespoons olive oil
- 1 teaspoon chili powder
- 1/2 teaspoon cumin
- 1/4 teaspoon cayenne pepper
- Salt to taste

Instructions:

1. Preheat your oven to 400°F (200°C).
2. In a bowl, toss the chickpeas with olive oil, chili powder, cumin, cayenne pepper, and salt until evenly coated.
3. Spread the chickpeas in a single layer on a baking sheet.
4. Roast in the preheated oven for 30 minutes, stirring occasionally, until crispy and golden.
5. Let cool slightly before serving.

Nutritional Information (per serving):

- Calories: 210
- Protein: 10g
- Carbohydrates: 30g
- Fat: 7g
- Fiber: 8g

Grilled Vegetable Skewers

Preparation Time: 20 minutes (plus marinating time)
Cook Time: 10 minutes
Number of Serves: 4

Ingredients:
- 1 zucchini, cut into rounds
- 1 yellow squash, cut into rounds
- 1 red bell pepper, cut into chunks
- 1 green bell pepper, cut into chunks
- 1 red onion, cut into chunks
- 16 cherry tomatoes
- 1/4 cup olive oil
- 2 tablespoons balsamic vinegar
- 1 garlic clove, minced
- Salt and pepper to taste
- Wooden or metal skewers

Instructions:
1. In a large bowl, whisk together olive oil, balsamic vinegar, minced garlic, salt, and pepper to make a marinade.
2. Add the chopped vegetables to the bowl and toss to coat evenly. Let marinate for at least 30 minutes.
3. Preheat the grill to medium-high heat.
4. Thread the marinated vegetables onto skewers, alternating types for variety.
5. Grill the skewers for about 10 minutes, turning occasionally, until the vegetables are tender and lightly charred.
6. Serve hot.

Nutritional Information (per serving):
- Calories: 150
- Protein: 2g
- Carbohydrates: 12g
- Fat: 11g
- Fiber: 3g

Zucchini and Corn Fritters

Preparation Time: 15 minutes
Cook Time: 20 minutes
Number of Serves: 4

Ingredients:

- 2 cups grated zucchini (about 2 medium zucchinis)
- 1 cup corn kernels (fresh, frozen, or canned)
- 1/2 cup all-purpose flour
- 1/4 cup grated Parmesan cheese
- 2 green onions, thinly sliced
- 2 eggs, beaten
- Salt and pepper to taste
- Olive oil for frying

Instructions:

1. Place the grated zucchini in a colander, sprinkle with salt, and let stand for 10 minutes to draw out moisture. Squeeze out the excess water.
2. In a large bowl, combine the drained zucchini, corn kernels, flour, Parmesan cheese, green onions, and beaten eggs. Season with salt and pepper, and stir until well mixed.
3. Heat olive oil in a large skillet over medium heat. Scoop 1/4 cup of the mixture per fritter into the skillet, flattening slightly with a spatula.
4. Cook the fritters for about 3-4 minutes on each side, or until golden brown and crispy.
5. Transfer to a paper towel-lined plate to drain any excess oil. Serve warm.

Nutritional Information (per serving):

- Calories: 220
- Protein: 9g
- Carbohydrates: 23g
- Fat: 11g
- Fiber: 3g

Olive and Tomato Tapenade

Preparation Time: 10 minutes
Cook Time: 0 minutes
Number of Serves: 4

Ingredients:

- 1 cup pitted Kalamata olives
- 1/2 cup sun-dried tomatoes, drained if oil-packed
- 2 tablespoons capers, rinsed
- 1 garlic clove
- 1/4 cup olive oil
- 2 tablespoons fresh lemon juice
- Salt and pepper to taste
- Fresh basil leaves for garnish

Instructions:

1. In a food processor, combine the Kalamata olives, sun-dried tomatoes, capers, and garlic. Pulse until coarsely chopped.
2. With the processor running, gradually add the olive oil and lemon juice, processing until the mixture becomes a coarse paste.
3. Season with salt and pepper to taste. Transfer to a serving bowl and garnish with fresh basil leaves.
4. Serve with crusty bread or crackers.

Nutritional Information (per serving):

- Calories: 190
- Protein: 1g
- Carbohydrates: 6g
- Fat: 18g
- Fiber: 2g

Sweet Potato Wedges with Herbs

Preparation Time: 10 minutes
Cook Time: 30 minutes
Number of Serves: 4

Ingredients:

- 2 large sweet potatoes, cut into wedges
- 2 tablespoons olive oil
- 1 teaspoon dried rosemary
- 1 teaspoon dried thyme
- Salt and pepper to taste

Instructions:

1. Preheat your oven to 400°F (200°C). Line a baking sheet with parchment paper.
2. In a large bowl, toss the sweet potato wedges with olive oil, rosemary, thyme, salt, and pepper until well coated.
3. Arrange the wedges in a single layer on the prepared baking sheet.
4. Bake in the preheated oven for about 30 minutes, turning halfway through, until the wedges are golden and crispy.
5. Serve warm.

Nutritional Information (per serving):

- Calories: 180
- Protein: 2g
- Carbohydrates: 24g
- Fat: 9g
- Fiber: 4g

Marinated Artichoke Hearts

Preparation Time: 10 minutes (plus marinating time)
Cook Time: 0 minutes
Number of Serves: 4

Ingredients:

- 1 can (14 ounces) artichoke hearts, drained
- 1/4 cup olive oil
- 2 tablespoons white wine vinegar
- 1 garlic clove, minced
- 1 teaspoon dried oregano
- 1 teaspoon dried basil
- Salt and pepper to taste
- Fresh parsley, chopped for garnish

Instructions:

1. In a bowl, whisk together the olive oil, white wine vinegar, minced garlic, oregano, basil, salt, and pepper to create the marinade.
2. Add the drained artichoke hearts to the marinade, tossing gently to coat.
3. Cover and refrigerate for at least 2 hours, or overnight for best flavor, stirring occasionally.
4. Before serving, garnish with fresh parsley. Serve chilled or at room temperature.

Nutritional Information (per serving):

- Calories: 150
- Protein: 2g
- Carbohydrates: 6g
- Fat: 14g
- Fiber: 3g

CHAPTER 7: DESSERTS

Baked Apples with Cinnamon

Preparation Time: 10 minutes
Cook Time: 30 minutes
Number of Serves: 4

Ingredients:

- 4 large apples, cored
- 4 teaspoons unsalted butter
- 4 teaspoons honey or maple syrup
- 1 teaspoon ground cinnamon
- 1/4 cup chopped walnuts or almonds (optional)
- 1/4 cup raisins (optional)

Instructions:

1. Preheat your oven to 350°F (175°C).
2. Place the cored apples in a baking dish.
3. Fill each apple's center with 1 teaspoon of butter, 1 teaspoon of honey (or maple syrup), a sprinkle of cinnamon, and if desired, some chopped nuts and raisins.
4. Pour a small amount of water into the bottom of the baking dish to prevent the apples from sticking.
5. Bake in the preheated oven for 30 minutes, or until the apples are tender.
6. Serve warm, with the syrup from the baking dish spooned over the apples.

Nutritional Information (per serving):

- Calories: 160
- Protein: 0.5g
- Carbohydrates: 34g
- Fat: 4g
- Fiber: 5g

Berry and Yogurt Parfait

Preparation Time: 10 minutes
Cook Time: 0 minutes
Number of Serves: 4

Ingredients:

- 2 cups Greek yogurt
- 2 cups mixed berries (strawberries, blueberries, raspberries, blackberries)
- 4 tablespoons granola
- Honey or maple syrup to taste (optional)

Instructions:

1. In serving glasses or bowls, layer 1/4 cup of Greek yogurt followed by a layer of mixed berries.
2. Sprinkle 1 tablespoon of granola over the berries.
3. Repeat the layers until the glasses are filled, ending with a layer of berries.
4. Drizzle with honey or maple syrup if desired.
5. Serve immediately or chill until ready to serve.

Nutritional Information (per serving):

- Calories: 180
- Protein: 12g
- Carbohydrates: 24g
- Fat: 4g
- Fiber: 3g

Almond and Orange Flourless Cake

Preparation Time: 15 minutes
Cook Time: 45 minutes
Number of Serves: 8

Ingredients:
- 3 cups almond flour
- 1 cup granulated sugar
- 1 teaspoon baking powder
- 3 large eggs
- Zest of 1 orange
- 1/4 cup fresh orange juice
- 1 teaspoon vanilla extract
- Powdered sugar for dusting (optional)

Instructions:
1. Preheat your oven to 350°F (175°C). Grease and line an 8-inch round cake pan with parchment paper.
2. In a large bowl, mix together the almond flour, granulated sugar, and baking powder.
3. In another bowl, whisk the eggs, orange zest, orange juice, and vanilla extract until well combined.
4. Gradually add the wet ingredients to the dry ingredients, stirring until just combined.
5. Pour the batter into the prepared cake pan and smooth the top with a spatula.
6. Bake in the preheated oven for 45 minutes, or until a toothpick inserted into the center comes out clean.
7. Let the cake cool in the pan for 10 minutes, then transfer to a wire rack to cool completely.
8. Dust with powdered sugar before serving, if desired.

Nutritional Information (per serving):
- Calories: 320
- Protein: 10g
- Carbohydrates: 28g
- Fat: 20g
- Fiber: 4g

Dark Chocolate Sea Salt Almonds

Preparation Time: 10 minutes
Cook Time: 5 minutes (plus setting time)
Number of Serves: 4

Ingredients:

- 1 cup whole almonds
- 6 ounces dark chocolate, chopped
- 1/2 teaspoon sea salt

Instructions:

1. Line a baking sheet with parchment paper.
2. In a double boiler or microwave, gently melt the dark chocolate, stirring until smooth.
3. Add the almonds to the melted chocolate, stirring until they are completely coated.
4. Using a fork, lift the almonds out of the chocolate one by one, tapping off any excess chocolate, and place them on the prepared baking sheet.
5. Sprinkle the chocolate-coated almonds with sea salt while the chocolate is still melted.
6. Allow the chocolate to set completely at room temperature or in the refrigerator before serving.

Nutritional Information (per serving):

- Calories: 300
- Protein: 6g
- Carbohydrates: 18g
- Fat: 24g
- Fiber: 4g

Grilled Pineapple with Honey Drizzle

Preparation Time: 5 minutes
Cook Time: 10 minutes
Number of Serves: 4

Ingredients:

- 1 pineapple, peeled, cored, and cut into rings
- 2 tablespoons honey
- 1 teaspoon cinnamon

Instructions:

1. Preheat a grill or grill pan to medium-high heat.
2. Grill the pineapple rings for about 4-5 minutes on each side, or until they have nice grill marks and are slightly caramelized.
3. Warm the honey in a small saucepan over low heat or in the microwave for a few seconds.
4. Arrange the grilled pineapple rings on a serving platter, drizzle with warm honey, and sprinkle with cinnamon before serving.

Nutritional Information (per serving):

- Calories: 120
- Protein: 1g
- Carbohydrates: 32g
- Fat: 0g
- Fiber: 2g

Lemon and Olive Oil Sorbet

Preparation Time: 15 minutes (plus freezing time)
Cook Time: 5 minutes
Number of Serves: 4

Ingredients:

- 3/4 cup sugar
- 1 cup water
- 3/4 cup fresh lemon juice (about 3-4 lemons)
- 1 tablespoon lemon zest
- 3 tablespoons extra virgin olive oil

Instructions:

1. In a small saucepan, combine the sugar and water. Heat over medium heat, stirring until the sugar has dissolved. Let the syrup cool to room temperature.
2. Once cooled, stir in the lemon juice, lemon zest, and olive oil.
3. Pour the mixture into an ice cream maker and churn according to the manufacturer's instructions until it reaches a sorbet consistency.
4. Transfer the sorbet to a freezer-safe container and freeze until firm, about 2-3 hours, before serving.

Nutritional Information (per serving):

- Calories: 200
- Protein: 0g
- Carbohydrates: 35g
- Fat: 7g
- Fiber: 0g

Poached Pears in Red Wine

Preparation Time: 10 minutes
Cook Time: 30 minutes
Number of Serves: 4

Ingredients:

- 4 ripe pears, peeled, halved, and cored
- 2 cups red wine
- 1/2 cup sugar
- 1 cinnamon stick
- 1 strip of orange zest
- 1 vanilla pod, split lengthwise (or 1 teaspoon vanilla extract)

Instructions:

1. In a large saucepan, combine the red wine, sugar, cinnamon stick, orange zest, and vanilla pod. Bring to a simmer over medium heat, stirring until the sugar dissolves.
2. Add the pear halves to the saucepan. Reduce the heat to low, cover, and simmer gently for 20-30 minutes, or until the pears are tender but not falling apart.
3. Carefully remove the pears from the liquid and set aside.
4. Increase the heat to medium-high and continue to cook the liquid until it reduces by half and becomes syrupy, about 10-15 minutes.
5. Serve the poached pears drizzled with the red wine syrup.

Nutritional Information (per serving):

- Calories: 250
- Protein: 1g
- Carbohydrates: 50g
- Fat: 0g
- Fiber: 5g

Fig and Ricotta Tart

Preparation Time: 20 minutes
Cook Time: 35 minutes
Number of Serves: 8

Ingredients:
- 1 pre-made pie crust or tart dough
- 1 cup ricotta cheese
- 1/4 cup honey, plus more for drizzling
- 1 teaspoon vanilla extract
- 8-10 fresh figs, sliced
- 1 tablespoon lemon zest
- Powdered sugar for dusting (optional)

Instructions:
1. Preheat your oven to 375°F (190°C). Roll out the tart dough and press it into a 9-inch tart pan with a removable bottom. Prick the bottom with a fork. Bake for 10 minutes, or until lightly golden.
2. In a bowl, mix the ricotta cheese, honey, and vanilla extract until smooth.
3. Spread the ricotta mixture evenly over the pre-baked tart shell.
4. Arrange the sliced figs on top of the ricotta in a circular pattern, starting from the outside and working your way in.
5. Sprinkle the lemon zest over the figs and drizzle with a little more honey.
6. Bake in the preheated oven for 25-30 minutes, or until the figs are juicy and the edges of the tart are golden brown.
7. Let the tart cool before removing it from the pan. Dust with powdered sugar before serving, if desired.

Nutritional Information (per serving):
- Calories: 280
- Protein: 6g
- Carbohydrates: 35g
- Fat: 14g
- Fiber: 2g

CHAPTER 8: 28-DAY MEAL PLAN

Week 1

Day 1
- **Breakfast:** Seafood Frittata
- **Lunch:** Shrimp Mango Ceviche
- **Dinner:** Octopus and Potato Salad

Day 2
- **Breakfast:** Smoked Salmon Avocado Toast
- **Lunch:** Lentil Salad with Cod
- **Dinner:** Mussels in White Wine

Day 3
- **Breakfast:** Berry Chia Pudding
- **Lunch:** Simple Seafood Paella
- **Dinner:** Shrimp Asparagus Stir-Fry

Day 4
- **Breakfast:** Oatmeal with Poached Pear
- **Lunch:** Portuguese Fish Stew
- **Dinner:** Sea Bass with Olive Salsa

Day 5
- **Breakfast:** Mackerel and Sweet Potato Hash
- **Lunch:** Mediterranean Tuna Pasta Salad
- **Dinner:** Cod in Tomato Chickpea Sauce

Day 6
- **Breakfast:** Greek Yogurt with Honeyed Walnuts
- **Lunch:** Grilled Sardine Bruschetta
- **Dinner:** Creamy Seafood Risotto

Day 7

- **Breakfast:** Quinoa Berry Breakfast Bowl
- **Lunch:** Tuna Niçoise Salad
- **Dinner:** Herb-Crusted Hake

Week 2

Day 8

- **Breakfast:** Spinach and Feta Scrambled Eggs
- **Lunch:** Crab and Avocado Wrap
- **Dinner:** Clam and Kale Soup

Day 9

- **Breakfast:** Shrimp and Avocado Salad
- **Lunch:** Haddock in Parchment with Vegetables
- **Dinner:** Grilled Swordfish with Quinoa

Day 10

- **Breakfast:** Sardine and Tomato on Wholegrain
- **Lunch:** Salmon and Quinoa Salad
- **Dinner:** Baked Salmon with Roasted Veggies

Day 11

- **Breakfast:** Greek Yogurt with Honeyed Walnuts
- **Lunch:** Mediterranean Tuna Pasta Salad
- **Dinner:** Creamy Seafood Risotto

Day 12

- **Breakfast:** Spinach and Feta Scrambled Eggs
- **Lunch:** Shrimp Mango Ceviche
- **Dinner:** Sea Bass with Olive Salsa

Day 13

- **Breakfast:** Berry Chia Pudding
- **Lunch:** Salmon and Quinoa Salad
- **Dinner:** Herb-Crusted Hake

Day 14

- **Breakfast:** Smoked Salmon Avocado Toast
- **Lunch:** Tuna Niçoise Salad
- **Dinner:** Baked Salmon with Roasted Veggies

Week 3

Day 15

- **Breakfast:** Seafood Frittata
- **Lunch:** Simple Seafood Paella
- **Dinner:** Mussels in White Wine

Day 16

- **Breakfast:** Quinoa Berry Breakfast Bowl
- **Lunch:** Portuguese Fish Stew
- **Dinner:** Clam and Kale Soup

Day 17

- **Breakfast:** Sardine and Tomato on Wholegrain
- **Lunch:** Crab and Avocado Wrap
- **Dinner:** Shrimp Asparagus Stir-Fry

Day 18

- **Breakfast:** Mackerel and Sweet Potato Hash
- **Lunch:** Grilled Sardine Bruschetta
- **Dinner:** Octopus and Potato Salad

Day 19
- **Breakfast:** Oatmeal with Poached Pear
- **Lunch:** Haddock in Parchment with Vegetables
- **Dinner:** Cod in Tomato Chickpea Sauce

Day 20
- **Breakfast:** Shrimp and Avocado Salad
- **Lunch:** Lentil Salad with Cod
- **Dinner:** Grilled Swordfish with Quinoa

Day 21
- **Breakfast:** Greek Yogurt with Honeyed Walnuts
- **Lunch:** Mediterranean Tuna Pasta Salad
- **Dinner:** Creamy Seafood Risotto

Week 4

Day 22
- **Breakfast:** Spinach and Feta Scrambled Eggs
- **Lunch:** Shrimp Mango Ceviche
- **Dinner:** Sea Bass with Olive Salsa

Day 23
- **Breakfast:** Berry Chia Pudding
- **Lunch:** Salmon and Quinoa Salad
- **Dinner:** Herb-Crusted Hake

Day 24
- **Breakfast:** Smoked Salmon Avocado Toast
- **Lunch:** Tuna Niçoise Salad
- **Dinner:** Baked Salmon with Roasted Veggies

Day 25
- **Breakfast:** Seafood Frittata
- **Lunch:** Simple Seafood Paella
- **Dinner:** Mussels in White Wine

Day 26
- **Breakfast:** Quinoa Berry Breakfast Bowl
- **Lunch:** Portuguese Fish Stew
- **Dinner:** Clam and Kale Soup

Day 27
- **Breakfast:** Sardine and Tomato on Wholegrain
- **Lunch:** Crab and Avocado Wrap
- **Dinner:** Shrimp Asparagus Stir-Fry

Day 28
- **Breakfast:** Mackerel and Sweet Potato Hash
- **Lunch:** Grilled Sardine Bruschetta
- **Dinner:** Octopus and Potato Salad

CHAPTER 9: SUSTAINING THE ATLANTIC DIET LIFESTYLE

Beyond the 4-Week Plan

Starting the Atlantic Diet through the initial 4-week meal plan is just the beginning of an exciting path toward better health and well-being. As you move beyond the 4-week meal plan, you're stepping into a phase where the principles of the Atlantic Diet become a natural part of your daily life, allowing you to sustain and build upon the healthy habits you've developed.

Adopting a Lifelong Journey

Congratulations on completing the 4-week meal plan! You've learned the basic principles of the Atlantic Diet, sampled a range of dishes, and started implementing positive changes in your eating habits. Now it's time to transform these practices into a long-term lifestyle that improves your health and happiness.

Customizing Your Dietary Choices

Your unique preferences, needs, and lifestyle are central to maintaining a healthy diet. Feel free to customize recipes to your liking, experiment with local and seasonal ingredients, and creatively incorporate the Atlantic Diet's principles into every meal, whether you're eating alone, with family, or at a social gathering.

Advancing Your Meal Planning Skills

Building on the foundational meal planning skills you've developed, this next phase encourages you to dive deeper. Learn how to batch cook effectively, experiment with new flavor combinations, and tailor your meal planning to fit a busy schedule, ensuring that healthy eating remains convenient and satisfying.

Committing to Continuous Learning

The realm of nutrition and culinary arts is large and constantly evolving. Retain your curiosity and willingness to experiment with new ingredients, culinary techniques, and recipes. Cooking classes, food blogs, and healthy eating communities can help you improve your culinary skills and inspire delicious, nutritious meals.

Practicing mindfulness and moderation

Mindful eating—savoring each bite, listening to your body's indicators, and enjoying meals without distractions—can greatly improve your relationship with food. Embrace moderation in portions and indulgences, striking a balance that allows for occasional treats without derailing your dietary requirements.

Integrating Physical Activity

A balanced lifestyle extends beyond what you eat. Discover physical activities that you genuinely enjoy and make them a regular part of your routine. Whether it's a brisk walk, a swim, or a yoga session, moving your body is crucial for complementing the dietary benefits of the Atlantic Diet.

Building and Leaning on Your Support Network

You are not alone on this journey. Connecting with others who share similar goals can provide invaluable support, motivation, and a relationship. A solid support network, whether it is family, friends, or online communities, can be crucial to your success.

Reflecting on Your Journey and Setting New Goals

Take some time to reflect on your accomplishments, challenges, and learnings. Setting new, attainable goals—whether for dietary habits, physical activity, or overall well-being—can help you remain focused and motivated. Remember that growth is not linear, and every step forward is a win.

Adapting Meal Prep to Life's Changes

This concept explores the capacity to stay dedicated to the Atlantic Diet amidst life's inevitable fluctuations. This is designed to equip you with strategies that extend beyond the kitchen, concentrating on the flexibility of your meal planning routine in response to life's dynamic nature.

Embracing Change with Creativity

Life's changes often present new opportunities for culinary creativity. As your circumstances evolve, so too can your approach to meal prepping. This might involve exploring new ingredients that become available as a result of a move or change in local markets, or experimenting with different cooking methods if your living situation changes. The key is to view these changes as an opportunity to reorganize your meal prep routine and infuse it with new flavors and experiences.

Simplifying For Busy Periods

Simplicity is especially important during busy times. Focus on meals that require minimal preparation and cooking time but still adhere to the nutritional principles of the Atlantic Diet. Consider assembling rather than cooking, utilizing fresh, raw ingredients to create meals like salads with canned fish, fresh fruits, and nuts, which can be prepared quickly yet are loaded with nutrients and flavor.

Expanding for Family and Friends

Life's celebratory moments often revolve around meals shared with family and friends. These events necessitate expanding your meal preparation to accommodate larger events, which can provide an opportunity to showcase the Atlantic Diet's adaptability and appeal. Plan meals that are scalable and easily customizable to accommodate additional people, ensuring that you can enjoy the company without compromising your dietary values.

Adjusting to Dietary Needs

Changes in health or dietary preferences, whether personal or within your family, require an adaptable meal prep strategy. The Atlantic Diet's emphasis on whole meals and an extensive variety of ingredients makes it inherently adaptable. Learn how to substitute ingredients to cater to new dietary demands, ensuring that each meal remains healthy, balanced, and consistent with the diet's key principles.

Integrating Local and Seasonal Changes

As seasons change, so do the available ingredients. Incorporate local and seasonal vegetables into your meal planning to embrace the seasonal rhythm. This not only brings diversity to your meals, but it also helps you connect with your local environment and community. Seasonal eating can rejuvenate your meal preparation routine and encourage you to create dishes that reflect the flavors of the season.

Nurturing Resilience Through Routine

Establishing a resilient meal prep routine means developing habits that can withstand life's ups and downs. This means setting aside regular time for meal planning and prepping, even when life gets hectic. It's about finding balance and making meal planning a non-negotiable part of your week, so you always have nutritious meals available no matter the circumstances.

Staying Motivated and Inspired

"Staying Motivated and Inspired" focuses on the mental and emotional aspects of maintaining an effective eating pattern. This focuses on cultivating a positive mentality and finding continuous inspiration in your journey, ensuring that your passion for this dieting technique remains consistent over time.

Cultivating a Positive Mindset

The key to staying motivated is to cultivate a positive attitude toward meal preparation and healthy eating. Viewing meal prepping as an opportunity for creativity and self-care, rather than a chore, can change your perspective. Celebrate minimal wins, such as mastering a new recipe or noticing improvements to your health, to establish a positive connection to your meal prepping routine.

Setting Achievable Goals

Setting specific, attainable goals can provide direction and a sense of purpose in meal prepping. Whether it's trying a new recipe each month, incorporating a wider variety of vegetables into your meals, or polishing your cooking skills, goals give you milestones to strive for and celebrate, keeping your motivation high.

Seeking New Inspirations

Seek new sources of inspiration on a regular basis to keep your meal prep journey exciting. This could include exploring cookbooks, food blogs, or social media channels dedicated to the Atlantic Diet or similar cuisines. Engaging with a community of like-minded people can also provide a plethora of inspiration and ideas, allowing you to expand your culinary horizons.

Connect with Your "Why"

Reminding yourself of the reasons you chose to follow the Atlantic Diet can serve as a powerful incentive. Whether your "why" is health-related, environmental, or based on a desire for gastronomic discovery, reconnecting with your initial motivations can reignite your enthusiasm for meal planning, especially when the excitement has decreased.

Embracing Variety

Variety in your meal prepping is essential to avoiding monotony while keeping your meals exciting. Experiment with different food products, cuisines, and cooking methods while sticking to the framework of the Atlantic Diet. Seasonal changes provide a natural rhythm for introducing variety, making sure your meals are both delicious and diverse.

Reflecting and adjusting

Regular reflection on your meal prep journey allows you to recognize what works effectively and what might need to be adjusted. This continuous process of reflection and adaptation ensures that your meal prep routine continues to meet your evolving needs and preferences, keeping you engaged and inspired.

CHAPTER 10: CONCLUSION

As we reach the end of this guide to Atlantic Diet meal prepping, we reflect on the journey taken, not just through the pages of a book, but through the life-changing process of adopting a lifestyle deeply rooted in the traditions and richness of the Atlantic regions. This subject matter has not only exposed you to a variety of flavors and techniques, but also encourages you to incorporate a comprehensive approach to eating into your daily life.

This path represents a commitment to wellness, sustainability, and the joy of sharing meals that nourish both body and soul. You've been provided with the information required to make informed food choices, understanding the nutritional importance of fresh, seasonal produce, and the profound impact of a diet rich in seafood, whole grains, and vegetables.

This book aims to elevate the conventional concept of meal preparation, transforming it from an exhausting chore to a meaningful ritual that celebrates the richness of life. It's about finding beauty in simplicity, embracing life's changes, and modifying your cooking routines to keep your diet balanced and satisfying.

The Atlantic Diet's principles support a broader narrative of sustainability and respect for the environment. By choosing local and seasonal foods, you contribute to creating a more sustainable food system that values the health of our environment as much as our own. This path is as much about personal health as it is about contributing to a collective movement towards a more sustainable future.

Looking forward, the end of this book is merely the beginning of your ongoing adventure with the Atlantic Diet. The horizon is filled with endless opportunities for exploration, progress, and enjoyment. Continue discovering new recipes, experiment with diverse ingredients, and share the joy of healthy eating with those around you.

FAQs on the Atlantic Diet

This section aims to demystify this diet by addressing common questions and providing clear, thoughtful answers. It's an invaluable tool for people who want to know more about the Atlantic Diet and how they can integrate it into their everyday lives.

What is the Atlantic Diet?

The Atlantic Diet is a dietary pattern inspired by the traditional eating habits of coastal regions surrounding the Atlantic Ocean, primarily in Portugal and Spain. It prioritizes fresh seafood, whole grains, fruits, vegetables, legumes, nuts, and olive oil, mirroring the Mediterranean diet's focus on whole foods and healthy fats.

How does the Atlantic Diet differ from the Mediterranean Diet?

The Atlantic Diet, like the Mediterranean Diet, emphasizes whole foods and healthy fats, however, it places a greater emphasis on seafood owing to the coastal communities' access to fresh fish and shellfish. It additionally comprises a wider variety of seaweeds and marine vegetables, reflecting the Atlantic Ocean's unique biodiversity.

Is the Atlantic Diet suitable for weight management?

Yes, the Atlantic Diet can be conducive to weight management due to its focus on nutrient-dense, high-fiber foods that promote satiety and help regulate appetite. However, as with any nutritional pattern, portion control and mindful eating are necessary for achieving and maintaining a healthy weight.

Can I follow the Atlantic Diet if I have dietary restrictions or allergies?

Absolutely. The Atlantic Diet is quite customizable. For people allergic to seafood, lean poultry and plant-based protein sources can be used as replacements. Similarly, the diet's concentration on fruits, vegetables, and healthy grains makes it suitable for vegetarian and gluten-free diets, with appropriate substitution.

How can I start implementing the Atlantic Diet in my daily meal prep?

Begin by including more seafood into your meals, aiming for at least two servings per week. Gradually increase your consumption of whole grains, legumes, fruits, and vegetables, and use olive oil as your primary cooking and dressing fat. Planning your meals around seasonal vegetables could also help you adhere to the diet's principles.

Are there any specific cooking methods preferred in the Atlantic Diet?

The Atlantic Diet promotes cooking methods that maintain food's natural flavors and nutrients, such as grilling, baking, steaming, and sautéing. These approaches are consistent with the diet's emphasis on simplicity and healthfulness.

How can I stay motivated to stick with the Atlantic Diet?

Staying motivated requires diversity and community. Experiment with different recipes and ingredients to keep your meals interesting. Additionally, sharing the experience with friends or family members, whether by cooking together or sharing Atlantic Diet-inspired meals, can improve your dedication and satisfaction.

Where can I find Atlantic Diet recipes?

This book has an extensive collection of Atlantic Diet recipes to help you get started. In addition, culinary websites, cooking blogs, and traditional cookbooks from Atlantic coastal regions can be helpful resources for expanding your recipe repertoire.

Printed in Great Britain
by Amazon